Papa's Spaghetti

Papa made spaghetti,
a pot of hot spaghetti.
He put it on the table.
"Here's your lunch,"
said Papa.

CHEESE

3

But Mama cried, "Oh Papa!
There's something wrong
with our lunch today.
There's a fly in our spaghetti!
A fly in our spaghetti!"

And Papa replied,
"Don't worry.
I'll send in a spider
to chase it away."

Then Tony cried, "Oh Papa!
There's something wrong
with our lunch today.
There's a spider
in our spaghetti!
A spider in our spaghetti!"

And Papa replied,
"Don't worry.
I'll send in a bird
to chase it away."

Then Anna cried, "Oh Papa!
There's something wrong
with our lunch today.
There's a bird
in our spaghetti!
A bird in our spaghetti!"

And Papa replied,
"Don't worry.
I'll send in a cat
to chase it away."

Then Michael cried,
"Oh Papa!
There's something wrong
with our lunch today.
There's a cat
in our spaghetti!
A cat in our spaghetti!"

And Papa replied,
"Don't worry.
I'll send in a dog
to chase it away."

Then Tina cried, "Oh Papa!
There's something wrong
with our lunch today.
There's a dog
in our spaghetti!
A dog in our spaghetti!"

And Papa replied,
"Don't worry.
I'll send in a lion
to chase it away."

13

Then Baby cried, "Oh Papa!
There's something wrong
with our lunch today.
There's a lion
in our spaghetti!
A lion in our spaghetti!"

And Papa replied,
"Don't worry.
I'll send in an elephant
to chase it away."

And everyone cried,
"Oh Papa,
NO MORE!"